# Let's Explore!

Written by Catherine Saunders

Penguin
Random
House

**Editors** Pamela Afram, Gaurav Joshi, Himani Khatreja
**Editorial Assistant** Beth Davies
**Art Editors** Lauren Adams, Karan Chaudhary, Dimple Vohra
**Assistant Art Editor** Pranika Jain
**DTP Designers** Umesh Singh Rawat, Rajdeep Singh
**Pre-Production Producer** Marc Staples
**Pre-Production Manager** Sunil Sharma
**Producer** Louise Daly
**Managing Editors** Simon Hugo, Chitra Subramanyam
**Managing Art Editors** Neha Ahuja, Guy Harvey
**Art Director** Lisa Lanzarini
**Publisher** Julie Ferris
**Publishing Director** Simon Beecroft

**Reading Consultant** Linda B. Gambrell, Ph.D.

Dorling Kindersley would like to thank Randi Sørensen, Paul Hansford,
and Lisbeth Skrumsager at the LEGO Group.

First American Edition, 2015
Published in the United States by DK Publishing
345 Hudson Street, New York, New York 10014

Page design copyright © 2015 Dorling Kindersley Limited
A Penguin Random House Company
15 16 17 18 19   10 9 8 7 6 5 4 3 2 1
001–279459–September/2015

A catalog record for this book is available from the Library of Congress.
ISBN: 978-1-4654-3684-9 (Hardback)
ISBN: 978-1-4654-3533-0 (Paperback)

DK books are available at special discounts when purchased in bulk for
sales promotions, premiums, fund-raising, or educational use. For details, contact:
DK Publishing Special Markets, 345 Hudson Street, New York, New York 10014
SpecialSales@dk.com

Printed in China.

# www.LEGO.com
# www.dk.com

A WORLD OF IDEAS:
**SEE ALL THERE IS TO KNOW**

# Contents

# Let's Explore

It's summer in Heartlake City and the sun is shining. Best friends Mia, Emma, Andrea, Stephanie, and Olivia want to spend their summer vacation doing something truly amazing every day.

Mia loves animals so she suggests exploring the Heartspring Mountains on horseback or helping her grandparents at the Sunshine Ranch. Emma wants them all to get creative, so she thinks they should find unusual corners of Heartlake City to photograph. Andrea is always busy so she would prefer to spend the summer chilling out at the City Pool or camping in the Whispering Woods.

Stephanie loves to organize everyone and wants them to travel to interesting new places in her convertible car or seaplane. Inventive Olivia thinks they should challenge themselves to make a new app or build a clever time-saving gadget. Will the friends ever agree on what to do this summer?

Emma, Olivia, Andrea, Stephanie, and Mia are a talented, independent, and adventurous group. Each girl has her own interests and passions, so they often have different ideas about what they should do together. When they can't agree on what to do, the girls call a group meeting in Olivia's tree house, discuss their ideas, and then take a vote. Best friends can always work things out!

The girls have been best friends for some time. Andrea, Stephanie, and Emma met when they played on the same soccer team, then Stephanie and Emma got to know Mia at summer riding camp. Olivia met the rest of the girls by accident. She had just moved to Heartlake City with her parents and didn't know anyone her own age. While dog-sitting, Olivia lost a puppy and had to go looking for her all over Heartlake City. Along the way, she met Emma, Andrea, Stephanie, and Mia, who all helped her find the puppy. The five girls have been best friends ever since.

The girls have very different personalities and dreams, but somehow they still get along very well. Andrea is a confident performer who loves to shine. She is a talented singer, dancer, and actress and dreams of becoming a famous pop star.

Emma is a creative genius and she sees beauty in everything and everyone. She wants to be an artist, fashion designer, photographer, or filmmaker—definitely something creative!

Olivia is super-smart and extremely practical. She loves making and fixing things in her workshop and might even become an inventor one day.

Mia is caring and kind. She adores animals and she hates to see them sick or injured. She would love to do something where she can help animals and plans on becoming a veterinarian or animal psychologist.

Stephanie is energetic and organized. She's a natural leader and dreams of having a job where she can make a difference, such as a TV producer or a newspaper editor.

# SUMMER PLANS

The vacation has begun and the girls want to make the best of their summer. What fun things should they do?

**Mia**

I'm going to help my grandparents take care of animals at the Sunshine Ranch.

**Stephanie**

All I can think about is where in the world I could travel to. I'm so excited!

**Olivia**

Livi the pop star is coming to town... Maybe she'll let me photograph her!

**Andrea**

The weather is so warm and perfect. Maybe I will head out to the woods and camp.

**Emma**

I want to do something creative like... design postcards!

It's the last day of school and Stephanie, Mia, Andrea, Olivia, and Emma can't wait to start their summer vacation. They have studied hard and finished all their homework, so now it's time to have some fun!

They will miss their teacher, Ms. Stevens, and all their school friends, but for now they are planning some awesome new adventures. And when these five girls get together, anything is possible.

As always, the girls get together to make plans. Stephanie calls a group meeting. She asks each girl to share her ideas on what they could do during the summer months. The girls have many great suggestions such as hiking, hot-air ballooning, surfing, shopping, makeovers, and mountain biking. The problem is, they will never be able to choose only one. Stephanie thinks they can do all of them! The others agree, so Stephanie suggests writing a list so they won't forget anything. Emma, Mia, Andrea, and Olivia burst out laughing. Stephanie is always super-organized—she just can't help it.

# Heartlake City

The girls can't wait for their summer adventures to begin. They think the best place to start is close to home. Heartlake City is the perfect mix of natural beauty spots, such as the Ambersands Beach and the Whispering Woods, and cool urban hangouts, such as the Heartlake Shopping Mall, Heartlake Skate Park, and the Heartlake Arena. No one could ever get bored in Heartlake City!

The people of Heartlake City are pretty amazing, too. From Emma's talented parents to Andrea's cool aunts, the girls have lots of family members around to inspire them. They also have some cool friends. Stephanie's friend Kate is always ready for an adventure, while Andrea's friend Noah has a head for heights. Mia's cousin Liza is eager to go exploring with the girls. There's even a rumor that the famous pop star Livi will visit the town. It looks like a busy summer for the girls.

# MAP OF THE CITY

Heartlake City is a bustling town. There is adventure around every corner—you just need to know where to look! Let's explore.

**Emma's Tourist Kiosk**
Visit Emma at the tourist kiosk for maps of Heartlake City or advice for getting around.

City Park Café

Olivia's House

Lake Heart

**Heartlake Vet**
The Heartlake Vet will treat any animal whether it's a large horse or a tiny hedgehog.

**Heartlake Hair Salon**
Need a new look? Visit this fabulous salon for a stylish makeover.

Heartlake High

Heartlake Juice Bar

Heartlake City Pool

**Skate Park**
Check out the brand-new skate park. You might just run into Mia!

Ambersands Beach

Heartlake Lighthouse

The first thing on the girls' to-do list is a trip to the Heartlake Shopping Mall—it was fashionista Emma's suggestion, of course. She wants to check out the latest trends and plan the girls' summer look. It needs to be practical, versatile, and, most of all, fabulous! Stephanie has come along, too. Andrea, Mia, and Olivia want sensible Stephanie to make sure that Emma doesn't pick out anything too crazy for them to wear.

Emma and Stephanie have a great time at the mall. Emma has found the perfect clothes and accessories for all her friends, so she thinks that she and Stephanie deserve a treat. A trip to the day spa would be perfect! While the girls take a well-earned break at the spa, they bump into one of

18

their favorite people—Olivia's aunt Sophie. She is the town veterinarian and is taking time out from her busy schedule. She has some good suggestions to add to the girls' list of summer plans. What could they be?

While Emma and Stephanie are busy shopping at the mall, Andrea puts her own plan to relax into action. She heads straight to the Heartlake Juice Bar for a refreshing drink and a catch-up with her friend Naya. Naya makes the best smoothies and juices in town—customers can't get enough of her Fruit Frenzy, Veggie Volcano, and Summer Surprise. Andrea chooses a Summer Surprise smoothie, which has a new flavor every day. Today Naya has created a mouthwatering melon drink. It is very healthy and so delicious!

Andrea and the other girls all think Naya is fabulous. She loves surfing, creating smoothies, and playing the saxophone. Andrea likes talking to her about music, and sharing her dreams for the future. Naya tells Andrea about her own dream of traveling the world and helping people. Andrea thinks that sounds amazing! Maybe when she is a famous pop star, she will travel the world, too, giving free concerts to all her fans.

Checking out Heartlake City's brand-new Skate Park is a high priority for Mia this summer. She has been skateboarding for a while now and is so excited that Heartlake finally has its own cool hangout for skate fans. She's been saving up for a new skateboard and can't wait to practice her jumps and flips on the ramps at the new park.

Mia thinks the Skate Park is awesome!
She can't wait to tell her boarding buddy
Matthew all about it. Mia's rescue puppy,
Charlie, likes to follow her everywhere, so
he comes to the Skate Park, too. Mia decides
that Charlie should learn how to skateboard,
so she gives him a ride on her new board.
Charlie loves it! So Mia swaps her board for
roller skates and lets Charlie have fun on
the skateboard. Mia also shows Charlie a
new trick she has learned—a half-pipe jump.
Charlie is so excited, he starts to bark loudly
and jumps up and down.

Olivia has spent a lot of time in her workshop, and could do with a little fresh air. She calls her friend Joanna and suggests that they head off on a camping trip. Joanna thinks it is a great idea, so Olivia packs some things in her caravan and attaches it to her car. She heads to Joanna's house and then picks up Andrea. Camping was Andrea's idea for summer activities.

Olivia heads toward Whispering Woods where the girls set up camp outside. The weather is so warm that they decide they are going to sleep under the stars. After a delicious meal cooked by Olivia, the girls settle down and look at the night sky. Of course, Olivia can name all the stars. As the girls relax a cute hedgehog named Oscar joins them.

Olivia and Andrea are not the only ones getting closer to nature. Mia is busy helping her grandparents at the Sunshine Ranch. Running a farm is hard work, but Mia doesn't mind. She loves taking care of the animals, and there are plenty of them at the ranch. First, she feeds and grooms horses Mocca and Blaize and their foal, Fame. Then, she brushes the rabbit, Cream, who has a long angora coat. Next, she collects the eggs laid by Clara the hen, and finally she feeds Cotton the newborn lamb some milk.

Mia's cousin Liza is visiting the ranch, too. While Mia helps out with the animals, Liza looks after the crops and vegetable plot. Liza's passion is gardening and she wants to enter her fruits and vegetables into the Heartlake Farm Show, so they need to be perfectly ripe. In between working hard, the cousins find time to catch up with each other. Liza loves hearing all about Mia's adventures with her friends.

This summer, Stephanie wants to get out and about to different places. Her friend Kate agrees, so they jump into Stephanie's convertible and head to Ambersands Beach for the weekend. It's a lively place during the summer, buzzing with surfers, swimmers, sailors, and picnickers. Stephanie has a little house that opens out right onto the beach. It's the perfect spot for some summer fun!

Kate loves all watersports, but her favorite is jet skiing. She loves to ride around the bay, waving to her friends on the beach. This year, Stephanie is learning how to windsurf. She thinks it looks really cool, but it's not as easy as she thought it would be—she keeps falling off! But Stephanie is a very determined person and she won't give up. By the end of the summer, she'll be a great windsurfer!

After a day of watersports, Stephanie and Kate head back to the beach house for a cool ice cream on the terrace.

# LIGHTHOUSE FUN

A new ice-cream parlor has opened in town—inside a lighthouse! Stephanie and her friend Kate head over to check it out. The selection of ice cream is supposed to be delicious. This is going to be fun!

There are so many flavors of ice cream to choose from.

Seals often perch on the rocks surrounding the lighthouse.

Kate has found a treasure map in the parlor. Ooh!

The lighthouse is a great place to watch a sunset.

Rowboat for water adventures

Flashing lantern guides ships away from rocks.

An ice-cream parlor in a lighthouse? Fun!

Caretaker's room

Kate wastes no time getting a kiwi-flavored ice-cream cone.

Flowers bloom in every season here

Andrea always aims high, whether it's putting on a showstopping performance, or taking on a new challenge. This summer, though, the sky really is the limit—she is taking a ride in a hot-air balloon. The only problem is that Andrea has to share her trip with Noah, who is new in town. Andrea thinks that Noah isn't really her kind of person—he's too quiet and shy—and she isn't sure that he will be much help piloting the hot-air balloon. Noah isn't too thrilled to be trapped in a tiny hot-air balloon with a dramatic diva like Andrea, either!

However, Andrea and Noah grow closer as they share an amazing trip over Heartlake City and stop for a delicious picnic by Clearspring Falls. They discover that they have more in common than they thought. Andrea learns that Noah plays the clarinet and knows a lot about music, while Noah realizes that Andrea is fun, hardworking, and very talented.

# Andrea's Checklist

✓ Check the weather forecast before flying. Bad weather = bumpy flight.

✓ Check that all the controls and gauges are in working order.

✓ Make sure you have enough fuel in the gas cylinders before liftoff.

✓ Plan your route. After all, once you're up there, most clouds look alike!

✓ Don't forget to carry binoculars to spot Heartlake City's famous buildings and landmarks.

**Gas Burner**
Keep a safe distance from the burners. They are hot.

**Balloon**
Check for holes and tears. Better safe than sorry!

**Gas Cylinder**
Always carry extra gas. It's good to have more fuel for long journeys.

# Hard at Work

Mia, Olivia, Stephanie, Emma, and Andrea have big plans for the summer, but the vacation won't just be about having fun. Whether it is earning money to pay for their adventures or just using their talents to help others, the girls will be hard at work, too.

Emma works at the Pet Salon, helping animals look and feel great. Occasionally she also works as a lifeguard, keeping the beaches of Heartlake City safe for swimmers.

Mia volunteers at the Heartlake Vet, and this
summer, she is also trying her hand at selling
refreshing lemonade and cookies. Stephanie
is also a budding businessperson thanks to her
mobile bakery stand. Andrea works at the
City Park Café and has her own blog, *Andrea's
Alley*. Olivia isn't sure where she wants to work
this summer. She may work at a library, but
she's a science fan, not a bookworm. Hopefully
she'll find her perfect job soon.

Sometimes Mia's friends joke that she prefers animals to people. But Mia is very serious about animals and she is determined to have a career that involves helping them in some way. She believes that every animal should be safe and well looked-after. She wants to spend her summer getting as much experience working with animals as possible. Mia has helped out at the Heartlake Vet many times and the town veterinarian, Dr. Sophie, thinks that Mia is a natural with animals. She seems to understand them and they trust her right away.

So, when Dr. Sophie needs someone to run a new pet clinic on the outskirts of town, she knows exactly who to choose. Mia will be perfect for the job! This clinic will deal with minor pet problems, such as injured tails or sore paws, and regular health checkups. Mia is excited—it is her dream job. Best of all, Emma has volunteered to drive the Vet Ambulance, so they will be working together.

# AMBULANCE ALERT

A poor hedgehog has fallen into a pothole. Ouch!
It's a good thing Emma has a well-equipped
Vet Ambulance. She speeds to the rescue and
arrives just in time to comfort the tiny creature.

Feeding
bottle
with milk

Injured
hedgehog

Lights flash in an emergency

Comfy bed for hurt animals

Side mirror

Headlight

Stretcher for carrying hurt animals

41

This summer, Andrea has a new animal project, too—her family has recently adopted a rescue puppy. He is named Max and he is super-cute, but he needs some urgent training. The stubborn puppy never comes when he is called and loves sleeping in the middle of Andrea's bed, leaving her no space at all! Divas need their sleep, so Andrea calls in an animal expert to help—Mia, of course!

Mia comes over to meet Max and immediately figures out his problems. As a rescue puppy, Max has never been trained, so he just doesn't understand how to behave. Plus, he is scared of being alone and that's why he likes to sleep on Andrea's bed. Mia suggests that a comfy puppy bed in Andrea's bedroom will solve Max's (and Andrea's) sleep problems.

Then Mia gets started giving Max some puppy obedience and agility training. He thinks it's great fun. Soon he will be ready for the Lake Heart Dog Showcase!

Mia might be Heartlake City's biggest animal fan, but Emma enjoys working with animals, too. She even has a part-time job at the Heartlake Pet Salon. Emma thinks that animals deserve to look and feel fabulous, just like people do. Joanna works at the salon, too, and the two girls work together to keep the animals happy. Joanna and Emma deal with a variety of animals, from cats with bad hair days and puppies in desperate need of pedicures to parrots whose feathers need freshening up and tortoises whose shells need shining. They handle every animal carefully, using specially formulated pet products.

Emma's best customer is her own poodle, Lady. The cute puppy comes to the salon once a week for a shampoo and blow-dry. Emma loves her puppy to look just as stylish as she does. In fact, Emma and Joanna are designing a range of eye-catching pet accessories for Lady to wear.

Emma is perhaps one of the busiest people in Heartlake City this summer. As well as keeping the local animals safe and stylish, she also works at the Tourist Kiosk. Emma thinks that Heartlake City is the best place in the world, so she wants to make sure that the visitors enjoy their time there. She sells everything tourists need—sunscreen, snacks, sunglasses, and even souvenirs.

But her best-selling items are postcards.
Emma actually designs the postcards herself,
using photographs she took of her favorite
places in Heartlake City. Sometimes, she
even mails them for tourists who ask nicely.

Emma's favorite part of her job is when
tourists ask her advice on the best places to
visit. She knows all the coolest places in
town and is happy to give recommendations.
She makes sure that she mentions City Park
Café, where Andrea works, and Stephanie's
famous Bakery Stand.

# WELCOME TO
## HEARTLAKE
# CITY
### LET THE ADVENTURE BEGIN!

**So many places to eat**

- City Park Café
- Stephanie's Pizzeria
- Heartlake Juice Bar

## So much to see

- Heartlake Lighthouse
- Heartlake Arena
- Heartlake Shopping Mall

## So much to do

- Beautiful beaches
- Heartlake Skate Park
- Hot-air balloon rides

For more information, contact the Heartlake Tourist Kiosk

Andrea works at the City Park Café all year round, but summer is her favorite time. The café is buzzing and full of people, but everyone is relaxed and happy. It is a popular place to hang out and customers come from far and wide to taste the owner Marie's famous home-cooked pies. In summer, Marie also creates delicious homemade ice-cream sundaes and yummy milkshakes. Marie has traveled all over the world, so her recipes are full of surprises. Try the zucchini and chocolate sundae; it sounds weird, but it works!

As a waitress, Andrea is kept very busy. She takes orders, carries plates of food, clears tables, washes up, and sweeps the floor. She doesn't mind, though—she's saving up all her tips for a showstopping outfit to wear at her next big show. Marie knows all about Andrea's dreams of being a world-famous singer and she sometimes lets Andrea perform for the customers. It's good practice for Andrea, and it's great for business.

Stephanie's mobile bakery has been such a success that she feels confident she knows how to run a business. So, when the owner of the Heartlake Pizzeria asks her to take over while she is on vacation, Stephanie doesn't hesitate. How hard can it be?

At first, Stephanie tries to use her baking expertise, but the customers aren't very happy with caramel or chocolate-chip pizzas. She realizes that she knows nothing about pizzas—in fact, she doesn't even like them!

Fortunately, Stephanie's friends help her out: Andrea finds a simple pizza recipe, Mia whips up a delicious salad, and Olivia checks the oven. Soon, delicious pizza smells are coming from the pizzeria, and with a little help from Andrea's social networking, customers decide to give Stephanie another chance. Stephanie has learned some important business lessons this summer— always research your business first, and don't be afraid to ask for help when you need it!

# 🍴 FOOD AND DRINK 🍴

# Recipe for Success

*Heartlake City Correspondent*

Picture Credit: Heartlake City Daily News

Pizza lovers have one more reason to celebrate —a schoolgirl named Stephanie is managing a pizzeria, tucked away in her quiet neighbourhood.

Stephanie's Pizzeria has become the hottest hangout in Heartlake City. The biggest hit on the menu is the delicious pizza cupcakes. These tiny treats look like regular cupcakes, but once you bite into them, they have a gooey, cheesy center.

People just can't get enough! Customers don't seem to mind waiting in long lines to grab a piece for themselves. Stephanie even has a few regulars who drop in every day.

Stephanie wouldn't reveal the secret recipe for her cupcakes but she did have this to say: "I love pizza and I love cupcakes, so I thought of combining the two. I never knew people would like it so much. I'm very excited."

We're excited for you too, Stephanie.

> **Ratings:**
> Food: 5/5
> Ambience: 4/5
> Value for money: 5/5

While she was out at Sunshine Ranch, Mia met Nate, the son of one of her grandparents' neighbors. Mia likes Nate—he's funny, interesting, and enjoys helping people. His parents run a flower farm, and he usually helps out there when he is not at school. However, this summer Nate is looking for a different kind of job. He asks Mia's advice, and she has a great idea: Andrea's Aunt Susan is about to reopen the Heartlake Grand Hotel, and he should ask her for a job. The Heartlake Grand Hotel is the coolest building in Heartlake City. Nate would love to work there!

So, Nate pays Aunt Susan a visit and she thinks he will be perfect as her new bellboy. A bellboy's job is to greet customers and carry their luggage

to their rooms. Nate thinks it sounds fun!
He can't wait to start—he will
wear a shiny new uniform and
meet interesting people.

GRAND HOTEL

*Come and work for the*
# HEARTLAKE GRAND HOTEL

## ARE YOU

- **Free for the summer?**
- **Happy to help?**
- **Friendly and polite?**

## We need you!

# Bellboy
# Wanted

**APPLY NOW!**

Mia has told the others about her new friend, Nate, and they can't wait to meet him. Andrea suggests that they check out the Heartlake Grand Hotel and meet Nate at the same time. Andrea's aunt has promised to show them around and let them try out some of the cool things to do there. Emma and Mia are too busy working, but Andrea, Olivia, and Stephanie have the day off so they all head to the hotel.

However, when they arrive, there is no bellboy to greet them. Where is Nate? Aunt Susan explains that they have nicknamed him "Find Nate" as he's always so busy helping guests with their problems that she can never find him! The girls laugh and head to the rooftop pool to relax and drink some smoothies. Later they go to the top floor and finally find Nate— he's helping the DJ there!

Olivia doesn't have a part-time job, but she is working hard. She is busy inventing, experimenting, and fixing things in her workshop. Her greatest invention so far is her pet robot, Zobo. She designed and built him herself, but he's not quite finished yet.

Olivia's friends think she is extremely talented—she just seems to understand how things work. Her skills can be pretty handy, too. When the oven won't work at the pizzeria, Stephanie calls Olivia to fix it; when Emma's Vet Ambulance breaks down, Olivia solves the problem; and when Mia needs a new kennel at the Vet Clinic, Olivia builds her one.

When Andrea's Aunt Susan hears about Olivia's skills, she asks her if she has any ideas for the Heartlake Grand Hotel. Of course Olivia does! She suggests video-chatting screens in all the guests' rooms, finger scans instead of room keys, a cool light show for the fountain, and robot bellboys that will never go missing!

Emma is Heartlake High's roving news reporter. Although school is finished for the summer, she is sure her viewers will want to keep up to date with the latest news. So, when she hears about the reopening of the Heartlake Grand Hotel, she calls her friend Andrew and they head over in their news van.

Today is the grand opening of the hotel and Emma is hoping for an exclusive story. However, when she arrives at the hotel, she finds that Aunt Susan has a huge problem—none of the bedsheets has arrived! Emma leaves the news reporting to Andrew and offers to help. She heads to a fabric warehouse and buys lots of fabulous material. With Olivia's help, and a couple of sewing machines, Emma creates unique sheets in a rainbow of colors. Now the Heartlake Grand Hotel has designer sheets! Better still, Andrew gets an exclusive interview with the person who saved the grand opening—Emma.

# On Tour

The rumors are true! Livi, the world's most famous pop star, is coming to Heartlake City. Stephanie, Emma, and Andrea are huge fans of Livi. They know the words to all her songs, have read every article written about her, and watched every TV show she has ever been on. They think Livi is the perfect pop star—fun, talented, independent, and she cares about how her fans feel. Mia and Olivia think she's cool, too, but they aren't super-fans like their friends.

However, it's Mia who meets Livi first. The pink-haired pop star is an animal lover and needs someone to walk her precious dog, Cookie, while she is in town. Mia gets the job and soon realizes that her friends were right about Livi. She is just like them—a down-to-earth girl who is just following her dream. Livi cares about the same things they do—helping other people and hanging out with her friends.

# LIVING IT UP WITH
# LIVI

By Special Correspondent, Olivia

★ ★ ★

The world's coolest popstar is in Heartlake City! Olivia catches up with Livi, as the superstar gets ready for Heartlake City's biggest pop concert.

QUESTION: Hi Livi, welcome to Heartlake City. Are you excited about your big concert?

ANSWER: It's great to be here. Heartlake City is so beautiful. I can't wait to sing for all my fans.

Q We can't wait either. Tell us about your music; how do you record all your songs?

A Whenever I have to record a song, I head right to the recording studio. I grab my guitar and have fun singing!

Q That sounds like so much fun! Don't you get tired traveling and performing?

A My tour bus is my home away from home. It has everything I need to relax and prepare for my concerts.

Q Wow! The bus sounds really cool. I wish our school buses were like that. Tell us a little about your concert. What's the performance going to be like?

A We have set up a big stage with lots of lights. The stage panels will turn and I'll jump out. The musicians are going to play the instruments while I sing my most popular songs. It's going to be lots of fun. I just know that everyone is going to have a great time.

It's not just Emma, Stephanie, and Andrea who are excited about Livi's visit—the whole town has Livi fever! Everywhere they go, the people of Heartlake City are humming Livi's songs, talking about her show, and wondering what the glamorous pop star is really like.

When Emma visits the hot new Heartlake Hair Salon, she not only gets a fabulous new hairdo, she also gets the inside scoop on the real Livi. Natasha, the super-cool owner of the salon, is Livi's hairdresser, too! When she arrived, Livi sent a limo to pick up Natasha, so the creative stylist could make Livi's hair look a cut above the rest. Natasha invented Livi's signature shade of pink and won't use it on anyone else—apart from a small stripe in her own hair.

Natasha tells Emma that Livi might be world-famous, but she's really just a kind, friendly, creative person who genuinely cares about the people around her.

Andrea, Emma, Mia, Olivia, and Stephanie are not just music fans, they have their own band, too. Mia plays the drums, Olivia plays keyboards, Stephanie plays electric guitar, Emma sings backing vocals and is in charge of their look, and Andrea is the lead singer—naturally! They love to write their own songs and perform them together.

When Livi hears one of the band's songs, she thinks it is fabulous. She doesn't know who wrote the song but she decides to sing it in her show at the Heartlake Arena.

When the girls find out that Livi likes their music, they are delighted. They can't wait to tell her that they wrote the song together. Maybe Livi would invite them to sing with her. Unfortunately, Livi is surrounded by people, so the girls can't get close to her. Then, Olivia has an idea: They all have tickets to Livi's show, so they can tell her there. The plan works and Livi invites the girls on stage to perform their song with her.

After the show, Livi invites the girls to
visit her dressing room. They can't believe
that a famous pop star wants to hang out
with them! Livi is so friendly and normal,
and she wants to find out all about them.

As they chat with Livi, the girls begin to realize that life on tour can get pretty lonely. But Emma can think of one part of Livi's life she would love for herself— her wardrobe!

Inside Livi's super-cool dressing room, there are rows of fabulous, glittery stage outfits, racks of amazing shoes, and trays of the most awesome accessories Emma has ever seen. And Livi says she is welcome to borrow anything she likes from her wardrobe.

For Mia, the best part of Livi's dressing room is the special doggy relaxation area for Cookie. Livi is her kind of person! When Livi reveals that she plans to stay in Heartlake City for a while, the girls are so excited. They can't wait to show her around!

Livi loves exploring Heartlake City and hanging out with her new friends. Being a pop star is hard work so she enjoys spending some time being just a "regular" girl. Emma has designed a disguise for her so she won't get recognized wherever she goes. It's great fun! Now Livi can do whatever she wants, such as volunteering with Mia at Page's Pets, selling cupcakes with Stephanie, or going shopping with Emma.

However, Livi doesn't have too much time to relax—she has a new album to record. Her new friends will help her: Stephanie will

organize the studio, Mia will take care of
Cookie, Emma will design an inspiring outfit,
and Andrea will help with singing practice.
Olivia offers to use her technical know-how to
make sure that Livi's songs sound perfect. Livi
thinks it's a great idea! So, Olivia fine-tunes
all the equipment and makes sure everything
works correctly as Livi records her new album.
Thanks to her friends, Livi sounds fabulous.

# LIVI
# LIVE!

Relive all the hits from Livi's recent Heartlake City show.

New album available online and wherever music is sold.

**Heartlake Times**
"A voice so new,
so dazzling!"

**Heartlake City Magazine**
"The album of
the year!"

Now that her new album is finished, Livi has to get back to the job of being a pop star. Her time in Heartlake City has been amazing and she'll never forget her new friends. She has had so much fun with them and they have shown her how important it is to take time out to be yourself. However, Livi knows that the best way to promote her new album is by going back on stage.

First, Livi must tell the world about her new album. That means hitting the red carpet, making TV appearances, and giving interviews. Livi makes sure she travels around in style in a luxurious limo. She also grants an exclusive interview to someone very special—Olivia. Olivia is a guest writer on Andrea's blog this week, and she asks Livi the one question on every fan's mind: What inspired her new album? Livi gives her a wink and reveals that it was inspired by some special new friends in Heartlake City…

Now that the world knows about her album, it's time for Livi to get out there and perform her new songs for her fans. She's going on tour again, and it's another sell-out! This time, though, Livi asks Andrea, Olivia, Emma, Mia, and Stephanie if they would like to travel with her. Of course they would love to—but only for a short time, as they already have many other plans for the summer ahead.

Being on tour is exciting. Livi gets to travel the world, sharing her music with all her fans. Stephanie and Mia join her on her tour bus for the first part of the tour. It is the coolest vehicle the girls have ever seen! It is huge and has everything Livi could possibly need while she's away from home. There's a spacious living area, comfortable bedrooms to sleep in, a mini-stage to rehearse on, and even a hottub to relax in. Mia and Stephanie love being on the tour bus, especially when Livi lets Stephanie drive it.

When Livi needs to travel long distances, she swaps her tour bus for a luxurious private jet. It can take her anywhere she wants to go, quickly and in style. However, it can get lonely without any other passengers to share the ride, so Livi asks Olivia and her friend Matthew to take a trip with her. The two friends quickly pack their suitcases before Livi has time to change her mind. It's the chance of a lifetime!

Matthew is a budding guitarist, so he's hoping to jam with Livi on the plane. Olivia is more interested in all the cool gadgets Livi has on the plane, and she wants to speak to the pilot and learn all about how planes work.

Traveling by private jet makes Olivia and Matthew feel very special. Livi is so great to hang out with and it's fun to be part of her tour. However, they are both secretly glad to get home again. After all, there's no place quite like Heartlake City!

# Living like a star!

Posted: Today

Hello! I just spent an entire week with Livi the pop star! Yes, you read that right! My friends and I met Livi at her concert. She sang one of our band's songs and invited us on stage to sing with her. She is so cool!

Livi makes it look so easy, but being a superstar is hard work. We helped her record her new album. It was an experience I will never forget. I can't wait for you guys to hear it!

Livi even invited us to go on tour with her! It was just for a short time, though. Her tour bus is huge and her private jet is even bigger. What an amazing week!

## Comments:

**Emma**
Posted: Just now

I LOVED Livi. She is fab!

**Mia**
Posted: 1 hour ago

I'll really miss Livi and her cute dog, Cookie.

**Home** | **About** | **Contact** | **FAQ**

A picture of me playing drums at the concert. It was a dream come true.

## About me

**Name:** Andrea

Budding singer, part-time waitress, full-time awesome

Click to read more

Livi looked fabulous on the red carpet. Emma helped her pick the dress!

## Previous Posts

▶ Writing music
▶ My new pet
▶ Animal rescue
▶ Summer vacation
▶ A big problem
▶ The perfect gift
▶ Lighthouse fun
▶ Balloon ride

# Jungle Adventure

Now that Livi has headed back out on tour, Emma, Mia, Stephanie, Olivia, and Andrea can get on with the rest of their plans for the summer. When Emma and Stephanie met

Dr. Sophie in Heartlake Shopping Mall, the veterinarian suggested that they help out with looking after animals at the Jungle Rescue Base. Emma and Stephanie think it is a great idea and their three friends agree. Mia is especially excited. In the jungle, she's sure to see lots of interesting animals!

Before heading out to the jungle, the girls have to prepare. Mia tells them all about the animals they will be looking after—what they eat, how to handle them, and where they like to live. Emma creates outfits that will keep them cool in the jungle, Andrea makes sure they have all packed enough sunscreen and Stephanie finalizes their travel plans. Finally, Olivia's mom, who is a doctor, gives them injections to make sure they stay healthy in the jungle.

# What to Pack

⟹ Mosquito repellent

⟹ Sunscreen

⟹ Sunglasses

⟹ First-aid kit

PASSPORT

HEARTLAKE

Don't forget your passport, Olivia!
Love, Mom
xoxo

HEARTLAKE
CITY

When the girls arrive at the Jungle Rescue Base, Dr. Sophie is there to welcome them. She is so pleased that they have come to help her. However, before she has time to show them around the base, she's called out on an emergency. The girls had better get used to that—the rescue base is a busy place and you never know what will happen next!

While Dr. Sophie is busy helping an animal in need, Mia, Andrea, Olivia, Emma, and Stephanie explore the base by themselves. It's amazing!

It has a fully equipped medical center, a cool slide and zip line, plus all the comforts of home—including a hot shower and kitchen. Andrea is pleased to see a wireless antenna, so she can keep her blog updated during the trip, via Wi-Fi. By the time Dr. Sophie returns, the girls have already settled in to the base. They are ready to start work!

# THE JUNGLE

The girls have left the comforts of Heartlake City and are having a great time experiencing the wild. The Jungle is the perfect place for them to make new friends, help animals in need, and learn how to survive in tough conditions.

Jungle Bridge Rescue Helicopter airlifts hurt animals

Jungle Tree Sanctuary

Laboratory to test "jungle" samples

Jungle Falls

Hambo River

Lifebelt for water rescue missions

Emma volunteers to take the first mission. An urgent message has come through to the Jungle Rescue Base: there has been a rockfall and a monkey is trapped in a cave. Emma is nervous, but excited—it might be scary out there in the jungle, but she is here to help. So, Emma loads a shovel and some medical supplies onto the First Aid Jungle Bike and rides off to the rescue. Thanks to the speedy motorcycle, Emma reaches the trapped monkey in minutes.

The poor animal is very scared. Emma remembers what Mia told her and speaks to the animal in a calm, gentle voice. She tells him that everything will be okay, she's going to dig him out of the cave. It's hard work, but Emma frees the monkey. She checks him over for injuries, but miraculously the animal seems to be unharmed. Emma gives him a banana and decides to name him Romeo. Romeo is so grateful to Emma for rescuing him that he climbs into the motorcycle's sidecar and heads back to the base with his new friend.

Hey Dad,

I'm just writing to check in with you. How are things at home? Tell mom that I am doing just fine in the Jungle. I am staying at an animal rescue camp in the middle of two waterfalls. It is beautiful!

I have so much to tell you. There is no TV or cell phone reception here. But you know what? I don't need these things. There is so much else to do. Every day is a new adventure. Just the other day, Emma rescued a monkey trapped in a cave. I try to stay at the camp as much as possible to take care of pets from nearby villages. I think I will become a veterinarian one day, just like Aunt Sophie.

Ok Dad, I have to go now. It's time to feed my animal friends.

Love you,
Mia

House no. 15,

Sunshine Street,

(Next to Heartlake City Bank)

Heartlake City

Bath time for Romeo! Isn't he cute?

The girls are proud of Emma for rescuing Romeo, and now it's Mia's turn to help out. Dr. Sophie knows that Mia has plenty of experience caring for animals so she asks her to look after the injured animals at the Jungle Tree Sanctuary. Mia can't wait to get started. The sanctuary is not just for sick animals, though. It's also a friendly place where jungle animals can just play together.

Today, Mia has four animals to take care of. First, there's Bobbi the lion cub. Bobbi is too young to go hunting, so she goes to the sanctuary to see what's happening there instead. Romeo the monkey is also staying at the sanctuary for a while. He likes to spend time with Emma and her friends. There is also a visitor from Heartlake City—Goldie the yellow warbler bird. There is so much for the girls to explore at the sanctuary. They could probably stay here for a while!

The next jungle mission requires someone who is good at solving practical problems. That's Olivia, of course, so she grabs her tools and sets off. A tiger cub is stuck near the Jungle Falls. The river is very strong there, so the poor little creature is in danger of being swept away and she can't swim! The cub is very frightened. Olivia assesses the situation with her logical, scientific brain and soon comes up with a plan —she will build a dam to divert the water. Easy!

Olivia decides to name the tiger Flame, because of her bright coat. While Olivia builds the dam, she tells Flame all about herself and her friends and their exciting adventures—she suspects that Flame is curious about the world, just like she is. By the time that the tiger cub is safely back on dry land, Olivia and Flame have become good friends. Olivia tells her friend to keep on exploring, but maybe next time, she should be a little more careful!

# Know Your Animals

The girls are helping so many animals that it is becoming difficult to keep track of them. It's a good thing Mia is so organized. She has made a fact sheet for the girls to fill in for every animal they rescue.

| | |
|---|---|
| **Name** | Tony |
| **Species** | Chameleon |
| **Fun fact** | Can change its color |
| **Likes to eat** | Insects |
| **Loves** | Going on boat rides |

| | |
|---|---|
| **Name** | Java |
| **Species** | Macaw |
| **Fun fact** | Talks to people! |
| **Likes to eat** | Nuts and seeds |
| **Loves** | Teasing Romeo |

| | | |
|---|---|---|
|  | **Name** | Romeo |
| | **Species** | Monkey |
| | **Fun fact** | Likes to play pranks |
| | **Likes to eat** | Fruit and leaves |
| | **Loves** | Stealing food from Java |

| | | |
|---|---|---|
|  | **Name** | Bobbi |
| | **Species** | Lion cub |
| | **Fun fact** | Likes being cuddled |
| | **Likes to eat** | Bones! |
| | **Loves** | Playing with her brothers |

| | | |
|---|---|---|
|  | **Name** | Bamboo |
| | **Species** | Panda |
| | **Fun fact** | Is learning to climb trees |
| | **Likes to eat** | Bamboo shoots |
| | **Loves** | Hugs from his mom |

While Mia, Olivia, and Emma are out rescuing animals, Andrea and Stephanie are very busy at the rescue base, too. Andrea is monitoring the lookout post, using the telescope to see if she can spot any animals in need. Stephanie is busy in the kitchen—rescuing animals is hard work, and the others are sure to be very hungry when they get back to the base.

Suddenly, Andrea spots a panda in distress. He's close to the base, so they need to get to him—fast. She radios Stephanie to tell her to stop what she's doing and get the first aid kit ready. They have a mission! Andrea slides down the zip line and the two girls climb into the rescue boat. Within minutes they've rescued the panda. The poor creature has lost his parents and been scratched by another animal. Andrea applies some antiseptic cream and Stephanie decides to call him Bamboo, after his favorite food. The girls promise to look after him at the base.

# JUNGLE RESCUE BASE

The girls' base in the jungle is far from their cozy homes in Heartlake City. But with animals running around, rescue missions to plan, and chores to do, the girls love every bit of it!

Watchtower for spotting animals in danger

Shower area

Zip line for a quick exit

Living area with a kitchen and bedrooms

Water slide

The base sits on a stream

Emergency first aid kit

Mobile medical station

After saving Flame the tiger cub, Olivia
wants to help other animals. So, when
Andrea hears over the radio that there is
an injured frog in need of rescuing, Olivia
volunteers to go and find him. She decides
that the quickest way to get to the frog is by
boat. She packs some medical supplies and
rescue equipment and climbs into the rescue
base's one-seater speedboat. Olivia is an
experienced speedboat driver as her family
has a boat back in Heartlake City. This
boat is a little smaller, but much faster.

In no time at all, Olivia locates the poor injured frog. He's got an injured leg and is resting on a lily pad. Olivia switches off the speedboat's motor and gently glides towards the injured amphibian. He's really glad to see her, and not at all scared. His name is Zip and he loves meeting new people. Olivia persuades him to use his uninjured leg to hop aboard her boat and then they zoom back to the base.

Olivia, Andrea, Stephanie, Mia, and Emma aren't the only ones volunteering at the jungle rescue base this summer—Mia's friend, Matthew, is there, too. Matthew and Mia share a passion for skateboarding, and a desire to help animals in need. When a distress call comes in to say that Blu, a baby bear, is trapped on a broken bridge, the two friends decide to team up and rescue him.

Mia climbs into the helicopter so she can search the jungle from the air, while Matthew heads out in the off-road jeep. They keep in contact via radio. Mia spots Blu first, and radios the directions to Matthew. The bridge is so badly damaged that even Olivia couldn't repair it—the only way to rescue Blu is using the helicopter. Mia hovers above Blu and slowly lowers a stretcher toward him. The brave bear climbs aboard and then Mia maneuvers the stretcher toward Matthew's jeep. Matthew gathers a relieved Blu to safety and they all head back to the base.

# STEPHANIE'S FLIGHT PLAN

Stephanie loves flying with Heartlake Airlines so much that she came up with her own tips for getting the best experience.

**Be on time** Arrive early at the airport. It comes with perks like no lines and great seats.

**Pack light** Take only what you need. Lugging around a heavy bag is no fun.

**Eat well** The food cart has all sorts of tasty treats. Their cookies are the best!

**Enjoy the entertainment** Bored of watching the clouds? Catch up on movies instead.

HLA

**Listen carefully** Attendants make important announcements about the weather.

**Buckle up** Stay seated during touchdown and strap yourself in. It could be a bumpy landing.

# Back in Heartlake

Mia, Olivia, Emma, Andrea, and Stephanie had a truly amazing time in the Jungle and would love to go back there next year. In fact, it has been a wonderful summer and there's still time to have a few more fantastic adventures!

Mia is off exploring in her new car. It's a cool blue two-seater and she is so proud of it. It runs on a special eco-fuel so it is kind to the environment. Today she is off to see Olivia, who has just invented a new smoothie maker and is giving away free smoothies.

When the smoothies run out, Mia and Olivia plan to join Emma, who is busy playing mini golf. Stephanie might come along later, but right now she's taking a trip to a famous wishing fountain. The others wonder what she might be wishing for! Andrea is too busy practicing for her next show to play mini golf, but the five girls will definitely be together tomorrow. They have something very special planned!

The summer vacation is almost over, but the girls just have time for one last day of fun. For once, they all agree on what to do—they should have a party! Emma suggests having a barbecue on the roof terrace at her new house. Stephanie, Andrea, Mia, and Olivia love visiting Emma's house—it's so cool.

Emma's mom, Charlotte, is an architect so she designed the house. It has loads of great features, such as a romantic balcony and a relaxing garden. Olivia particularly enjoys talking to Charlotte about construction. Emma's dad, Luis, is an interior designer, so he is responsible for making the house look so amazing inside. The girls like the family room best with the enormous flat-screen TV that's perfect for movie nights.

As the girls enjoy the home-cooked food they chat about the summer. They have visited some fantastic places and met some inspiring people. It's nearly time to head back to school, but they don't mind —they're already making plans for next summer!

Emma has had the best summer vacation with her friends. It has been a great adventure! This scrapbook is perfect to remember all of their amazing moments.

Heartlake Skateboarding Tournament

ADMIT ONE

Seat No. 27
Gate No. 5

Mia spent most of her summer practicing at the new skate park. What fun!

# My Summer

Andrea almost got lost in the Whispering Woods. It's a good thing she had this map.

Olivia left cute little notes for Flame, which she always chewed up. Haha!

Sleep tight Flame!

My amazing postcards were a big hit with the tourists. My stamps were quite popular, too!

This is Stephanie's wristband from Livi's concert. It was a rocking night!

# Quiz

1. Who wants to become an inventor one day?

2. Where does Mia teach Charlie to skateboard?

3. Who does Andrea share her hot-air balloon ride with?

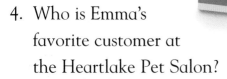

4. Who is Emma's favorite customer at the Heartlake Pet Salon?

5. What is the most famous dish served at the City Park Café?

6. What job does Nate get at the Heartlake Grand Hotel?

7. What does Mia like best about Livi's dressing room?

8. Who does Livi invite to ride with her in her private jet?

9. Where do the girls stay in the jungle?

10. Who looks after the animals at the Jungle Tree Sanctuary?

11. Where is Flame, the tiger cub, stuck when Olivia saves her?

12. What does Stephanie name the panda she saves?

13. What does Mia use to save Blu, while he is trapped on a broken bridge?

14. Which color is Mia's special eco-fuel car?

15. Who designed Emma's cool house?

See page 127 for answers

# Glossary

**Accessories**
A thing that can be added to something else to make it more useful or attractive.

**Agility**
The ability to move quickly and easily.

**Bay**
Where a sea or a lake curves into the land.

**Bookworm**
Person who loves reading books.

**Bustling**
Busy and lively.

**Clarinet**
A musical instrument made from a wooden tube.

**Convertible car**
A car with a top that can be raised, lowered, or removed.

**Fashionista**
A person who follows the latest fashion.

**Kennel**
A shelter for a dog.

**Luxurious**
Something that is very comfortable and usually expensive.

**Maneuver**
To move skillfully.

**Pedicure**
Scrubbing and cleaning feet and toenails to make them look beautiful.

**Practical**
Someone who is good at putting ideas or plans into action.

**Saxophone**
A musical instrument with a curved metal tube.

**Touchdown**
The moment when an airplane lands.

**Versatile**
Able to do many different kinds of things.

**Zucchini**
Long, thin, green vegetable.

# Index

Quiz answers:

1. Olivia  2. The Skate Park  3. Noah  4. Her poodle, Lady
5. Home-cooked pies  6. A bellboy  7. The doggy relaxation area
8. Olivia and Matthew  9. Jungle Rescue Base  10. Mia  11. Jungle
Falls  12. Bamboo  13. Rescue Helicopter  14. Blue  15. Emma's mom

# Have you read these other great books from DK?

## DK ADVENTURES

Jump into the action as heroes battle villains across the galaxy!

Find out all about the brave Jedi Knights and their epic adventures.

Emma adores horses. Will her wish come true at a riding camp?

Explore the amazing systems at work inside the human body.

Encounter the rare animals in the mountain forests of Cambodia.

Step back nearly 20,000 years to the days of early cave dwellers.